Against Principalities and Powers

ORBIS BOOKS

Maryknoll, New York 10545

AGAINST PRINCIPALITIES AND POWERS

LETTERS FROM A BRAZILIAN JAIL

Carlos Alberto Libanio Christo

Translated by John Drury

Originally published in 1971 as *Dai sotterranei della storia*

Second Edition, enlarged, 1973

Copyright © 1971 by Arnoldo Mondadori Editore, Milan, Italy

English translation copyright © 1977 by Orbis Books

Orbis Books, Maryknoll, New York 10545

Library of Congress Cataloging in Publication Data

Christo, Carlos Alberto Libanio, 1944–
    Against principalities and powers.

    Translation of Dai sotterranei della storia.
    Includes index.
    1.   Political prisoners—Brazil—Correspondence.
2.   Christo, Carlos Alberto Libanio, 1944–
I.   Title.
HV9593.C45513   365'.45'0924 [B]   76-43030
ISBN 0-88344-007-5
ISBN 0-88344-008-3 pbk.

We are contending against principalities and powers,
against the world rulers of this present darkness.
Therefore take the whole armor of God,
that you may be able to withstand in the evil day,
and having done all, to stand.

EPHESIANS 6:12–13

Contents

Foreword

The letters collected in this volume were written by Carlos Alberto ("Betto") Libanio Christo, theology student, member of the Dominican order, and formerly director of Student Catholic Action. After twenty-two months in prison awaiting trial, he was charged with participation in subversive acts and projects and sentenced to four years on September 14, 1971.

The letters need no commentary. Here I should simply like to recount some of the events leading up to Betto's imprisonment.

Carlos Alberto Libanio Christo was born in Belo Horizonte on August 25, 1944, into a middle-class traditional family from Minas Gerais, which is politically one of the most conservative states in Brazil. In Minas Gerais there began in March 1964 the movement that culminated in the military takeover of the Brazilian government. Upon completing secondary school, Betto moved to Rio de Janeiro. There he served as national director of the JEC,[1] the Young Christian Students movement, in its early efforts to infuse new life and Christian commitment into Catholic Action. In this work he collaborated with Bishop Candido Padim, who had early recognized the historical import of the new aspirations arising among Christian university students and teachers. Even then, in the early sixties, when most people still believed in the myth of "development," people in university circles were already exploring new and different ways to transform underdeveloped societies.[2] Betto enrolled in the school of journalism at the University of Rio de Janeiro, but he left the university in 1965 to enter the Dominican order. After his novitiate in Belo Horizonte, he took his first vows and then was sent to São Paulo in order to study philosophy. At the same time, he continued to take courses in communications and worked on the daily newspaper, *Folha de São Paulo*, to which he contributed articles on church renewal that proved exceedingly popular. In 1968 he made his solemn profession of vows, dedicating himself wholly to the religious life, and was sent to the state of Rio Grande do Sul to pursue his studies in theology at São Leopoldo Seminary.

There, on November 9, 1969, he was arrested by the Security Police on the charge that he had aided and abetted fugitive terrorists in crossing Brazil's southern frontier. In reality his arrest was part of a much wider campaign directed against the whole Dominican order in Brazil by the antiterrorist division of the special police services. On November 4, 1969, Carlos Marighella, the already legendary head of the ALN (Alliance for National Liberation), had been caught in a police ambush in the streets of São Paulo. Two Dominican religious were suspected of working with him, although their exact role is even now unclear. But it was enough to evoke broadcast accusations from the repressive police forces. In announcing that they had broken up a network of armed opposition, they claimed to have discovered working relationships between various guerrilla groups and members of the Dominican order. Nationwide arrests followed, from São Paulo to Rio Grande do Sul, where six priests and several dozen seminarians, including Betto, were arrested and imprisoned. Immediately the regime mounted an all-out propaganda campaign against these "terrorists." A nationwide investigation resulted in accusations against eleven Dominicans, two secular priests, and one Jesuit. The charge was involvement with the ALN "under the leadership of Carlos Marighella, carrying out administrative duties that offered aid and logistical support."

These charges furnished the excuse for an extensive campaign of vilification directed against the "progressive" wing of the church. Politically conservative factions urged the national episcopate to condemn "subversive" priests and bishops. The reaction of the hierarchy was at first ambiguous, but then Bishop Avelar Brandão, president of the Latin American Episcopal Conference, replying in the press, called the campaign a "premeditated plan to disparage the church," and his charge was picked up and repeated by the bishops of the Northeast. On November 19 the leaders of the Dominican order issued their own communiqué, which explicitly recognized "the sincerity of evangelical sentiment and the authenticity of love for their fellow human beings" of the imprisoned religious. Fourteen French Dominicans appealed directly to the Papal Commission on Justice and Peace, denouncing all statements that had been illegally extorted from the prisoners and emphasizing that the "Dominican Affair" could not be viewed separately from the fate of all Christians in Brazil who actively opposed government by oppression.[3]

All these statements, coming from people of widely differing outlooks, had one point in common: They appealed to the courts of justice. But in extraordinary circumstances such appeals are fruitless. Betto spent twenty-two months in prison *before* being sentenced, on September 14, 1971, to four more years in prison "without his guilt having been proven." This was the comment of Father Domingos Maia Leite, Provincial of the Dominican order in Brazil, to the press on hearing the sentence.

In prison Betto continued his theological studies, hoping ultimately to be ordained to the priesthood.

The gathering of the letters and their distribution in cyclostyle form was originally undertaken by Betto's parents. In their foreword to the letters, dated February 9, 1971, they wrote:

> We offer this selection of letters to those who are not familiar with the things he has written to us and to his friends. To follow his thinking through these letters is to discover who he is. He is here fully, for here one can see the motives and passions that guide him: love for others, a passion for justice, respect for human dignity, fidelity to the values which God entrusted to humankind so that we might prove worthy to perform the work of creation. Parents of this son whom we love and of whom we are proud, we believe that nothing more is needed to make him known to the reader acquainted with them. These letters tell you who and what he is, and they are enough to console us for the tremendous injustice he now suffers because of his love for the church.

The Italian version of these letters was based upon one of the cyclostyle sets, collated wherever possible with the original manuscript. For the safety of the persons involved, the names of the addressees have been omitted in many instances; but names of family members are given. Where the reader finds (. . .) in the text, a passage has been omitted because it concerns the author's private affairs or because it might bring harm upon another person. In a few places the hand of the prison censor has been indicated. Needless to say, all the letters passed through the hands of the prison censor.

For obvious reasons, Betto himself has not had any contact with the publisher or editor of this book. He does not know how the letters have been arranged, he has not seen the proofs, and he is in no way responsible for their publication in book form.

Linda Bimbi

In the English edition we have numbered the letters, and an index of major themes has been added at the end of the book. Thus readers may follow Betto chronologically through his years in prison by reading the text straight through, or they can discover Betto's views on a particular subject by consulting the Index. When a letter is addressed to the same person as the letter immediately preceding, the name of the addressee is not repeated.

Special thanks are extended to Naomi Noble Richard for her assistance in the preparation of the English translation.

Abbreviations

ALN   Alliance for National Liberation. Organization based on the Cuban model, established in 1967 under the command of Carlos Marighella.

CELAM   Latin American Episcopal Conference.

CICOP   Catholic Inter-American Cooperation Program.

DOPS   Department for Political and Social Order. There is a branch in each state of the Brazilian Federation.

FAB   Brazilian Air Force

IAPI   Social Welfare Institute (Brazil).

JEC   *Juventude Estudiantil Catolica.* Catholic student movement open to students below university level.

JUC   *Juventude Universitaria Catolica.* Catholic student movement for university students.

NASA   National Aeronautics and Space Administration (United States).

NATO   North Atlantic Treaty Organization.

UNE   National Students' Union (Brazil).

VPR   People's Revolutionary Vanguard. A splinter group of the Brazilian Communist Party, commanded by Captain Lercaro.

1

To Virgilio, a fellow seminarian
(shortly after Betto's arrest)

Porto Alegre
November 15

(. . .) The Holy Spirit blows where and when he wills. I'm deeply touched by your kindness and generosity, and I thank you and your friends. I remain united with you all in faith and joy.

"How blest are those who have suffered persecution for the cause of right." I embrace you warmly.

2

Porto Alegre
November 16

(. . .) Alleluia. Read John 15:18–22 and 16:1–4, the reading in today's Mass. It has been the subject of my meditation today.[4]

3

*To a group of young Christians
in Porto Alegre*

Porto Alegre
November 17

My dear friends, nothing new has happened here. We spend our time reading, praying, and dealing with little details that acquire great importance when you are in prison. It's like the life of a Carmelite. I have my Office here and try to pray the various Hours. I pray our heavenly Father that all this will have some meaning for the manifestation of his kingdom.

Come when you can. Everything suggests that I'll be here for a bit. I embrace you all. Let us remain united in the faith and joy of the Lord.

4

Porto Alegre
November 18

Dear Friends, thanks for everything you have done for me. I've just gotten out in the sunshine for a while. It was a fine change of scenery. (. . .) Yesterday evening we celebrated Mass here in prison. It was all very simple: Jesus here with us, our comforter and liberator.

Right now I don't need anything except the things I asked for in my note. (. . .) Please get in touch with my parents, Antonio Carlos and Stella, rua Padre Odorico 162, Belo Horizonte, telephone 22-0799.

Let us remain united in the joy of the Lord. I am here to carry out his will. Everything is grace.

I embrace you in friendship and gratitude.

5

To Virgilio

Porto Alegre
November 21

(. . .) We are well in the profound joy of the Spirit. We are grateful to be allowed to re-enact in our own lives Jesus' way to redemption. He was persecuted, imprisoned, and condemned. Shouldn't a Christian imitate his Master? We fear nothing. Jesus was calumniated, threatened, and betrayed by one of the Twelve. We are free because our freedom comes from within and no one can take it from us.

Pray for us and for the church because a new hour may well be here, the hour of "the church in prison."

In the joy of faith and the Resurrection.

6

To his sister Teresa

DOPS, Porto Alegre
November 25

Dear Teresa, this is my first letter to you from prison. I have been here for two weeks now, and I probably will be here for a long time to come. I have committed no crimes. My crime was to try to be a Christian in the true sense of the word. My crime was not to accept injustice, not to stoop to compromise with privilege. My crime was to help those who are in trouble risking their lives.

I'm not afraid. I have no regrets. I spend my days reading, thinking, and dedicating myself more to prayer. I live in complete inner freedom, content to believe that I am sharing in the mystery of Jesus Christ who was persecuted, imprisoned, and condemned for the sake of our freedom.

Time will make everything clear. I hope you all are well. (. . .)

7

To his parents

São Paulo
November 27

Dearest Mom and Dad, look beyond the factual details of what has happened. Disregard the reports and conjecture in the press. Disregard the accusations against me. Only one thing is important right now: I am in jail, and it is a source of joy to me. As the Bible tells us, what is wisdom in the eyes of human beings is folly in the eyes of God, and what is wisdom in the eyes of God is folly in the eyes of human beings. My arrest should cause you no shame but pride, as it does me. I am content. My conscience is at peace because what I said and did was in the interest of a more just world and a freer earth. With so much injustice around us it's not surprising that I find myself here.

I have not felt one moment of discouragement in prison. In fact I find it a truly enriching experience. Here you learn many things and become more of a realist. In particular you discover that a person is not judged by what he does in the sight of others but by what he is within himself. I am convinced that freedom of movement is not the whole meaning of human freedom. There are cloistered monks who are completely free, and no one is free who has not yet encountered himself. Prison makes possible this encounter with oneself and with others. It leads us to explore the infinite riches of the mind and spirit.

In Porto Alegre they decreed preventive detention for me, but I learned that the trial will take place in São Paulo. Everything indicates that the whole matter will be concluded rather quickly, the president of the Republic being among those who want it that way. Our lawyer here is Mario Simas, whom I met briefly at DOPS headquarters.

I believe that my visiting hours are from one to four o'clock on Wednesday afternoons. Anyone outside my immediate family who wishes to visit me must get a permit from Judge Nelson of the Second Military Court. I'm told that no formalities are required to obtain the permit.

As for letters, please write as often as you wish and can. Thanks for the hippy shorts. Shorts are our usual dress here.

Here in prison I met Doctor Madeira, who treated me when I had hepatitis. He's been in prison for ten months and is now the prison doctor, in fact if not by official decree. He's a marvelous person.

I embrace the two of you and all our friends. Let us remain united in prayer that God's will, not ours, be done.

A big hug to everyone, with much trust and affection.

8

(. . .) The only news here is my new prison life. Since I only arrived here a week ago, everything is still new to me. It's likely that I will be in Tiradentes Prison for some time.[5] There are about two hundred of us political prisoners here, young people of both sexes. Our cell is big, roomy, and airy. We have two bathrooms with showers, a washtub, and a kitchen with stoves. There are thirty-two people in our cell, almost all of them young. The few older men have adapted perfectly to their new style of life. We have two injured people. One was beaten up by the police when they seized him; the other threw himself out of a fourth-floor apartment window. Both are convalescing now. The group is divided into teams, which take daily turns at housekeeping. Yesterday it was my team's turn. We got up early, swept the cell, and made coffee (with milk and bread and butter). Some members of our team helped bathe the injured, while others did the cooking. I was a cook and by some miracle did not do too badly.

Occupations: French lessons, gymnastics, yoga, theology, conversations. When you have a strong spirit, prison life is tolerable. No one here seems to be unnerved or beaten down. Everyone is taking it in stride. The interrogations are finished, thank God. Now we must make the best possible use of our time here. I do not consider this time in prison a hiatus in my life. It is the normal continuation of it, and I feel keenly that I am going through a great experience (. . .).

9

Tiradentes Prison
December 13

Dear Family, Teresa has passed on to me the marvelous letter that you wrote me. It was a great source of encouragement in this difficult period. I am particularly touched by the fact that you have faced up so admirably to the ordeal of my imprisonment.

Yesterday, after I was formally sentenced to preventive detention, I was transferred from DOPS to this penitentiary. So I'm now reunited with the other Dominicans who were arrested. We are together with six other young men in a special cell. It is roomy enough, and we are a real community. We share everything we have and everything we receive. There is a stove in the cell, and we do our own cooking. A different group prepares the meals each day. I can assure you that the meals are delicious and varied.

I was at DOPS for two weeks. The first week was taken up mostly with interrogations, some of which were lengthy and exhausting. After some time and much explanation, the police were convinced that I was not so dangerous as I had been described or as the press had alleged. I am simply a Christian, and I am here precisely because I am trying to be a real one. When I realize that I belong to the church, that I, like you, am a member of Christ's mystical body, I feel proud that now I am sharing in body and spirit the situation (grace) of all those who sow the seeds of the gospel in the world. When he became man, God too was persecuted, taken into custody, tortured, and condemned to death. Paul was imprisoned for three years in Caesarea and for another two years in Rome. Peter, the leader of the apostles, was arrested in Jerusalem together with John. John was exiled to Patmos, where he wrote the book of Revelation. Stephen, James, and Simon were condemned to death in Jerusalem. In short the church to which we are joined by baptism has never been a conformist church, a rich and privileged church enjoying the favor of the powerful. It has been the church of the poor and the persecuted, the church of those who fight for justice, the church of those who act according to the Spirit rather than according to the law. Read the Acts of the Apostles. You will see that I'm right. I am very pleased that you read the Bible before meals. I will share your readings from here.

During my first week at DOPS, I was kept in solitary confinement in quite an uncomfortable cell. Then I was transferred to another cell, where I met eleven other prisoners. Most of them were young people and students. It's incredible how many university students are in prison! There were also a priest, an engineer, a dentist, a doctor, and a lawyer.

There is a great apostolic task to carry out in prison, so I do not regret being here. My only mission is to proclaim the good news of Jesus Christ. Everyone shows interest in my faith, in Christian doctrine, and in the religious life. They ask thousands of questions. It seems to me that our long chats shed some new light and help correct the distorted image many people have of Christian life and of the church.

At the same time, I am discovering here in prison young people who, though they are not religious, are living in a state of true holiness. They are pure, sincere, and wholly dedicated to their fellow human beings. They are always ready to lend a helping hand, to work for the group, and without counting the cost. I'm sure that the Spirit of God dwells in their hearts, which are full of vitality and goodness. I'm happy that God has granted me the grace to live in my own body the redemptive mystery of Jesus who, for his love of justice, was persecuted, imprisoned, and condemned to death.

Here I live with complete inner freedom. "What does it profit a man if he gains the whole world and then suffers the loss of his soul?" We used to see this gospel passage on the altar at Padre Machado,[6] if you remember.

I know that my imprisonment is a sign in the Brazilian church. I feel sure that all this is part of God's plan. Trust in him and let me play my part, just as you are admirably playing yours. He will reward us.

10

São Paulo
December 25

(. . .) We had a liturgical service with hymns and readings from the Bible. We don't celebrate Mass because the examining judge has not authorized it [censored].

I realize what this Christmas represents for our family. I'm sure that something is being born inside us, something that will bring us closer to the poor infant of Bethlehem. The Jews were waiting for a king, for the promised Messiah who would liberate Israel. Well the Messiah and king came, but without the trappings of human glory and temporal power. The authority of Jesus, the model of all authority, is that of a servant rather than a master. Christ is king because he is a servant. His birth has brought about a series of "signs of contradiction." In the life of faith no one reaches the Absolute except by passing through the insignificant.

Our family Christmas today recalls the mystery of a God who manifested himself as a poor baby in a manger. Prison is the place for evildoers, for thieves, vagrants, and criminals. It is the home of those who have been outlawed from society. Our penal system is not correctional, merely punitive. Our prisons do not reform; they corrupt and degrade. It is our honor, our glory, and our joy that our new life can be born in this "manger." But not everyone can understand this, just as not everyone can understand the mystery of the carpenter's son who suffered between two thieves. Only by the light of faith or the power of a profound ideal are such mysteries comprehensible. That is why those who have put us into prison cannot understand why we remain content, strong, and optimistic even here. We will never give them the satisfaction of seeing us sad or downcast.

I give thanks to our Father in heaven because you have grasped all this. If I have surprised you by my behavior in prison, you have surprised me much more by your capacity for

10

understanding and affection. I am surprised, not because I expected something different, but because God has chosen our family to participate in his plan of redemption in this way. Why us and not others? Why me and not someone else? The grace in our hearts prompts us to hope that future events will prove the rightness of our way. There is no victory without a struggle (. . .).

11

To his brothers and sisters

São Paulo
December 25

(. . .) Yesterday we had visitors from noon to five o'clock. Counting the relatives and friends of the more than one hundred prisoners here, at least a thousand people must have come. Some priests came from the monastery. Teresa[7] came too, bringing cigarettes and food. The prisoners' families got to know each other. Unfortunately it rained all day, which put a bit of a damper on the visit, but despite that the prevailing mood remained festive and gay. Our pantry is now chock full. Yesterday evening we had a kind of banquet, all thirty-four of us in this cell. We had chicken, turkey, baked rice, dried fruit, and grapes. We and the prisoners in the other cells sang together. There was no wine because alcoholic beverages are not permitted, so we had to settle for tap water.

Our lawyer came to see us. He has forwarded an appeal to the Supreme Military Tribunal, requesting that we be freed on bail. I don't think the request will be considered until after the first of the year. It's certain, however, that I would not enjoy the benefits of any such grant because of the accusations against me. But there is reason to hope that our case will not drag on forever. I've heard that the president of the Republic has ordered it to be handled quickly. I myself am in no great hurry. I'll be able to pursue my theological studies in prison, so I will not be wasting any time. It's just as if I were holed up in the seminary, completely absorbed in my studies. But I enjoy an additional advantage here: I'm closer to you, and I have other Dominicans to keep me company.

A hug for all our friends and relatives. I pray for everyone, and I'm grateful to those who have stood by you in this difficult time. I wish you a happy New Year, full of peace and joy.

1970

12

To his parents

São Paulo
January 5

(. . .) Unfortunately we were not permitted to have Mass on Christmas or New Year's Day. It seems unbelievable that, in a country that calls itself Christian, prisoners cannot participate in our Lord's sacrifice. But no one can stop us from praying and thanking God for enabling us to share the experiences of his Son in our lives.

I can't tell you how happy I am to know that dad went to Holy Communion. That is the best Christmas gift our family could receive. I prayed for it many years. Now the Lord has answered our prayers. We are living a perpetual Christmas because we are being born to new life in the Spirit. I would willingly endure other prisons so that other families might know the same grace.

Last year I meditated a great deal on the mystery of the Eucharist. Jesus instituted it in his last meal with his apostles, when he told them of the sufferings he would have to endure for our redemption. He took into his hands those most ordinary of foods, bread and wine, and he consecrated them: "This is my body which will be given up for you. This is my blood which will be shed for you. Do this in memory of me." What is the meaning of these words that we repeat at every Mass? Do they simply mean that the consecration of the Mass is performed in memory of Jesus' sacrifice? No, they do not mean

15

simply that. It is true that the Mass makes his sacrifice present here and now. But it also summons us to repeat Jesus' redemptive acts so that we might truly be imitators of him. When the priest repeats Jesus' words and gestures in the Mass and says, "Do this in memory of me," I interpret it as Jesus saying to us: "I have loved you completely, so much that I willingly died for you. I have given all that I am to free you. Having nothing left but my life, I did not grudge that either. I gave it up to show you that the limits of love are to love without limits. I have given you my body and blood. I have made this gesture a sacrament so that at any time or place in human history you may receive and re-enact my life in your own. When I said, 'Do this in memory of me,' I did not mean that you should simply commemorate what I had done. I meant that you should do likewise, that you too should offer your body and blood for the redemption of humanity. Just as at Mass you receive my body and blood so in your lives you should offer up your own so that my acts may be always present in the world through you. If other human beings receive you in their lives even as you receive me in Communion, then you and I will be in communion with each other."

Unfortunately, many Christians do not realize that Mass is something to be lived rather than merely attended and that it is lived to the extent that we are willing to sacrifice ourselves for the liberation of human beings. This sacrifice is not suffering. It is *the supreme joy*. Why? Because in it we find love in all its transparency and we become *God's Sacrament in the world* (. . .).

13

To his family

January 12[8]

(. . .) Thanks for the stationery and for the notebook that we use to play our navy battle game. That's how Castro and I passed the time when the two of us were in separate cells at

DOPS headquarters. We shouted our moves to each other through the bars—"B-12," "B-8," "A-5"—and one guard thought we were speaking in code. In prison any unusual action or movement arouses suspicion. Sometimes the police are alarmed by a simple look or gesture. The other day, for example, we didn't have enough water in our cell. It was terribly hot and the cell was stifling. It was my turn in the kitchen, but I couldn't prepare anything because we had been given so little water. Suddenly the sky darkened—we don't see much of the sky here, to tell the truth. There was the rumble of thunder, and then it began to pour. We hung a little bucket on the end of a broom handle and stuck it through an opening to catch some rain water. But quickly a guard appeared at our cell to tell us to pull in the bucket, or else the guard on patrol outside might mistake it for some sort of signal and shoot it full of holes. The guards who patrol outside usually carry machine guns. They substitute ordinary rifles only on visiting days.

Last week they transferred our guards. I think they do it as a precaution, so that the guards don't become sympathetic to their prisoners. For the present, police from the larceny squad are here. The atmosphere is more oppressive, and security is stricter. But they haven't bothered us in our cells.

I did not hear the president's New Year's address, but I am waiting for the "facts." I dare not say "acts" for fear that they might be more of the kind already promulgated.[9] You're mistaken if you think that we owe our relatively decent treatment here to him. In fact we owe it to you, our families. The food they serve us here is intolerable. It is shipped here every day from the state penitentiary in huge canisters. We manage to eat decently only because our families send us food and we have a stove in our cell. We do our own cleaning up, and we get two periods of fresh air per week. I say "fresh air" rather than "sun" because we go out into the courtyard at stipulated times whether it's raining or not. The doctor who takes care of us is also a prisoner. Thus his services represent a saving for the government and an abuse of his professional status. The same holds true for the two dentists who are imprisoned here, one of whom is a university instructor. There has been a sudden interruption in their work, however, and we do not know why.

There is another more serious matter. Although we are prisoners of the Military Tribunal, people from DOPS often come and take one or another of us away for further interrogation. Those taken are kept at DOPS for days and may be tortured again, without judicial authorization and without their defense attorneys' knowledge. In short we live without any guarantees.

On the other hand there is on the books a decree passed by Café Filho[10] (number 38016, dated October 5, 1955) that spells out the criteria governing the treatment of political prisoners. This law guarantees us, among other things, recreation, visits from blood relations at any time, unobstructed delivery and posting of mail, and medical care by a private physician. None of these things has been permitted to us. We've sent an appeal to the court, asking compliance with this law. It doesn't seem to me that we have asked for much, but we have not yet received any replies nor has there been any change or improvement in the routine of prison life. I am telling you this so that you may form a more realistic picture of our situation. What is more, we are still forbidden to celebrate Mass. As a Christian, I do not want or expect special privileges in prison. In fact I can't really feel sorry for myself when I see so many fathers of families incarcerated here with no way of helping their loved ones or relieving their present misery. Many don't have the wherewithal to hire a lawyer. So here we all are, even though our guilt has not even been proven.

I believe it is useless to forward petitions to the government, which will show its true face when it passes formal judgment upon us. Read Paul's letter from prison to the Ephesians. I remain happy and at peace because I know I am here "for the growth and spread of the gospel." I pray that the Lord will make us instruments of his justice and peace.

Your letters do me a lot of good. Let us remain united in our faith and in our lives, both illuminated by the word of God.

P.S. 1: After dinner today some people from DOPS suddenly showed up to take away one of our fellow prisoners. Even though he is under the jurisdiction of the Military Tribunal, the Tribunal was not consulted. Even the prison warden did not know that one of his prisoners had been spirited away. DOPS wants to know where the prisoner's brother is. The brother is wanted for engaging in certain political activities. How would our fellow prisoner, who has been in jail for three months, know the whereabouts of his brother, who disappeared from his home about a week ago?

Our fellow prisoner got back around 5:00 P.M. His hands and the soles of his feet were swollen from whippings. His shoulders were bruised, and there were two red streaks from the cord they had wound around his neck. Doctor Madeira happened to be in our cell when the prisoner returned, and he saw it all. We immediately sent a protest to the warden, who said he would do something about it. But meanwhile the boy has been tortured.

P.S. 2: I think there is a pressing need to denounce, in the name of justice, the torture now going on in the prisons of Brazil. There are thirty-five people in our cell, and I am the only one who has not been subjected to physical torture. I have, however, been subjected to psychological torture, for I have been threatened and also forced to look on when other prisoners were being mistreated. If anyone in politics is interested in taking up this cause, we can readily provide him with relevant evidence and material. During the dictatorship of Getulio Vargas one lawyer, Sobral Pinto,[11] pleaded that political prisoners be granted the same protection we would readily give to animals. I think the same plea is very much in order today.

P.S. 3: If you have a chance, write to our friends down south and ask them to send me my things. All I really need are my books. Give my clothes to someone who can use them. It's not worth keeping them for me (. . .).

14

February 10

Dear Sister, I enjoyed your letter very much (. . .). The support and understanding of brothers and sisters in the faith are a great consolation. I feel that I am suffering for the sake of the gospel. The path of the church is that of its Master. As *Lumen Gentium* (no. 8) puts it, ''Just as Christ carried out the work of redemption impoverished and persecuted, so the Church is called to follow the same path. . . . '' Why shouldn't we joyfully choose to live out this same experience in our own flesh and spirit? Wasn't Jesus tortured and condemned to death? (. . .) I'm sure that the real consecration of my religious life is taking place in this prison. Isn't it what we prayed for many times during our novitiate, as we pondered the lives of the saints and asked God to let us be the last among human beings? (. . .)

Today, banned from society, locked up behind bars and guarded by soldiers, sharing my life with prisoners and criminals, I can feel the grandeur of this mystery. I now realize in my own flesh why the Lord chose to be poor when he came to proclaim our salvation, why he lived among sinners and accepted the accusations of the Pharisees against him.

I have no reason for sorrow or regret. I can only give thanks to God as I live through this continuing Lent and prepare for a truly great Easter. Under trees in the garden outside your school I was taught the catechism and prepared for my first Holy Communion. Today I feel sure that the simple notions of the gospel that I learned then are enough to help me live the mystery of faith and the life of charity in all simplicity. My parents and you nuns were God's instruments. Through you I came to know these truths, and now I try to live them as best I can.

Our Dominican community here in prison thanks you for your prayers. We know it is the only support on which we can truly rely. For our part we wish to be a sign and symbol of the church of the poor, the persecuted church mentioned in the Acts of the Apostles. The fact is that we Christians cannot live according to the law; we must live according to the Spirit. What is folly in the eyes of men is wisdom in the eyes of God.

A big hug for you and all the sisters in your community. The Dominican community in prison is joined to your community by grace and prayer as we joyfully await the approaching Easter season.

15

To his brother, Luiz Fernando

February 22

(. . .) I was so happy to see the photo of little Flavio.[12] I suddenly realized that I feel almost like a father to him. It is as if he were a part of me. Seeing him in good health, so happy and roly-poly and at the same time unaware of what the future holds in store, I felt strong enough to fight for him and his future. I want to participate somehow in the struggle for a better future for him. His life is much more important than mine. I am in the prime of youth, and I feel no weariness. It seems well worth the effort to live my life for the sake of the generations that will come after me. They have the right to expect a more just world, where people can regard each other as brothers and sisters and where the disgraceful thing we call prison will no longer exist.

Why do some human beings imprison other human beings, putting them behind bars as if they were wild animals? We can't answer that question unless we're willing to admit that we live in a primitive state. Though we have evolved materially, our moral and spiritual evolution has come to a standstill. We have not yet discovered the full power and richness of the human spirit. Perhaps the Eastern world perceives the spirit more clearly than we do. It's significant that all the great religions arose in the Orient. The West has only been able to produce refrigerators, cars, and missiles. We have become spare parts in the gigantic machinery of the industrial world,

21

parts to be discarded when we jam the machinery or spoil the rhythm desired by those in power. The fact is that none of us is free in this respect. In one way or another we all are victims of this consumerist society in which economic profit is the basic objective.

There is in me a sense of justice that keeps me from accepting all this as a normal state of affairs. It is not just or right. When I look around at the world and then at the picture of Flavio, I am ashamed that I cannot offer him something better. The justification for our struggle and our sacrifice is to be found in little Flavio, in the children of my fellow prisoners here, in all the children of this country who will learn in school that we are a free nation—just because a Portuguese monarch raised the cry for independence on the bank of a little river[13] (. . .).

16

To his family

February 22

(. . .) An official of *Operaçao Bandeirantes*[14] came and took him[15] away. This happened about a week ago. Why? No one could say, not even he as they were leading him away. We expected him to be back the next day, but he didn't return. Days went by, and still he did not return. He is there, in "that place" where many of our companions have been tortured. Even the military police themselves refer to it as "hell's annex." Today we were told that he tried to commit suicide. Again they have put him to the "parrot-perch" torture[16] and electric shock. In all likelihood they tried to "suicide" him by slitting his wrists. He was then taken to the military hospital for blood transfusions, and he is now in solitary confinement. No one can get to see him or even find out what is going on.

Yesterday the apostolic nuncio, Umberto Mozzoni, came to see us. He also tried to see him but could not. Today we all are silent. Tomorrow the same thing could happen to any one of us. We enjoy no protection, no guarantees. We are like the Jews under Nazism. Times change, but evil does not. Oppression takes new names and new forms, that is all. Our silence is like that of Mary before her son. It signifies rage at this egotistical world, but it also hopes for justice and trusts that love will have its "hour" and its chance. Have confidence in us. A big hug for all.

17

To a religious community

February 22

(. . .) It is a rainy and gloomy Sunday here. Now there are fifty of us in this cell, and we are trying to make the best of it. Many are sleeping on mattresses on the ground because there is no room for more beds. The silence reflects the darkness of this gray day. It is not the silence of tranquility or inner peace; it is a kind of suffocation. So many people together and so little talk. It's as if we wanted to scream but the sound dies in our throat, and we simply keep silent and wait. For what? I don't know. No one does. Waiting is a permanent part of life in prison. It's like waiting on a railroad platform, but here there is no train and no track. Our silence is heavy-hearted like the weather. We are like people who, being provoked, bide their time and store up energy to react and counterattack later. We can feel our own impotence. No one can help us, and we ourselves can do nothing. It isn't a dead end because we have not yet given in to discouragement. Nor is it hate because we have not yet given in to despair. Perhaps it's rage—patient, silent rage at the labyrinth of absurdity before us.

What did the Jews think about in the concentration camps, knowing they would soon die in the gas chambers? Perhaps they thought about nothing, just as many of us are doing right now. Perhaps they simply waited in silence, but not for anything in particular—not for death and certainly not for some miraculous release. Perhaps they were incapable of thinking

23

about the unthinkable or fearing the inevitable. Once people realize that nothing depends on them any longer, that their fear is no longer a symptom of resistance, then they have nothing to do but wait in silence (. . .).

18

To his brother, Luiz Fernando

February 26

(. . .) We had a cordial visit from the apostolic nuncio. We priests and religious spoke with him for about two hours. We described our plight, and it made a deep impression on him. We have no guarantees and no security. He pledged his solidarity with us and showed great interest and understanding. He told us that Paul VI knows about our situation and that the Vatican Justice and Peace Commission knows about the tortures. After our conversation he gave us a fine box of chocolates and packs of American cigarettes. He also gave us the papal blessing. We asked him to visit the other prisoners too because the church must concern itself with the plight of *all* prisoners, not just clerics and religious. The prison warden assembled all the inmates in our wing, and the nuncio spoke to them. He alluded to the torture, showing real understanding for all those who fight in the name of justice. Then he gave the papal blessing to all, "even to non-Christians because the blessing of the Holy Father never hurt anyone." We asked him to make sure that the church took an interest in the families of those political prisoners who are really poor. He promised to get in touch with *Caritas Internationalis*[17] concerning their plight.

Today Cardinal Scherer of Porto Alegre came to visit us. He brought me a hug from Mom and Dad, whom he had seen in Belo Horizonte. He visited every cell, listened to the accounts of torture, and saw C. in our cell. C. has been in a cast since September. He cannot move, and he lies in bed without medical care.

We begged the cardinal to have the church—the only institution in Brazil not controlled by the government—take action on behalf of political prisoners. The fact is that only the church can help us now, and even its range of action is limited by the civil and military authorities.

I know Tito well. He would never become so desperate that he would try to commit suicide. I'm sure they tried to "suicide" him. It has happened to many political prisoners in our great Brazil. Yesterday the nuncio tried to see him, but they wouldn't permit a visit. Tito is back in the solitary confinement that the Military Tribunal had lifted three months ago. Who is responsible for what is going on here? Some people here lived under Fascism and Nazism, and they say that the present Brazilian regime is no different insofar as mass extermination is concerned. Others lived under the New State[18] and, according to them, the present repression is on a par with the refined police tactics of Felinto Muller.[19]

Faced with such facts, we realize how justified our struggle is. Our only regret is that we have not done much more.

I myself am fine. I have begun my theological studies again, although the judge has forbidden certain books on specific themes. The prohibition against Mass remains in effect. Such a measure can be justified only by a government that is persecuting the church.

It seems almost certain that we will be shifted to Tremembe Prison in Taubate[20] around the end of March. This will make visiting even more difficult, and we get few enough visits as it is. Anyone from Belo Horizonte who wants to visit me will have to get authorization from the Military Tribunal. And they'll say: "That guy has already had too many visitors." If that happens, my would-be visitors should reply that I specifically made arrangements to see them that week, putting off other visitors for that reason, and that they have come a long way to see me, and so forth.

A Swiss newpaper has published a report on Brazil, describing the "affair" in which I am involved. One of the questions on the entrance exam for the school of journalism in São Paulo was: "Who is Padre Betto?" When I get out, I think I will apply for some important job. . . .

A big kiss to all, especially to little Flavio.

19

March 3

(. . .) Tito is back with us. He stays in bed or drags himself around, limping. He is recuperating from the terrible suffering he endured. He was tortured for three days: parrot-perch, electric shock, whippings, beatings. They even reached new heights of sadism, putting an electrode in his mouth. It was the intention of the army to interrogate all the Dominicans once again, because they felt our interrogators at DOPS had been in too much of a hurry. To escape the suffering they were inflicting on him and to make a public protest against such interrogation of political prisoners, Tito finally resolved to commit suicide. He had a razor blade, and he slashed the veins and arteries on the inside of his left elbow. He lost a lot of blood.

We have done all we can to get the church to issue a protest. It must take a stand on the grave situation in Brazil before it is too late. But the bishops are used to being on the defensive, and they prefer omission to risk. Maybe someone will have to die before the church will react (. . .).

Father Vincent De Couesnongle, representing the superior general of our order, came from Rome for a quick visit. He and our father provincial spent yesterday afternoon with us. They came into the cell to see Tito. De Couesnongle said that our case has had profound repercussions in Europe. Everyone is interested and asks questions about us. The superior general has received manifestations of support and solidarity from the highest church authorities in Europe. Rome's support is unqualified, even in the Secretariat of State.

The Bible shows us clearly that God speaks through events. John XXIII reminded us that we must scrutinize the "signs of the times" in order to understand and appreciate God's activity in history. I believe that the events in which we have been involved here, through no merit of our own, are due to the action of God's Spirit. God is speaking to the church of Brazil and the church of Latin America through what is happening to us. That is why I feel we have nothing to lose and why I trust in God's providence. Tito's case is a striking proof of it.

26

In all likelihood the final results of the investigation into our case will be handed over to the court on the tenth of this month. Then the charge will be drawn up. I ardently wish that this phase of the whole process is handled quickly. Once I know the final verdict, I will be able to plan out my life in prison a little better. I feel psychologically ready for whatever happens to me. Living here with young people whose sentences will certainly be upwards of twenty years, I feel that our case is almost laughable. They are supported only by the strength of their ideals, while I have the support of the church. Their calm is a challenge to us.

(. . .) As far as little Tony's[21] First Communion is concerned, I think it's better to educate him in the faith and then wait for him to express a desire for Communion. He shouldn't be confronted with an obligation. No one should be "prepared for First Communion" specifically, but rather formed in the Christian faith.

A big hug to you all. Let us await Easter in unity. Now is the hour of the Passion. Soon there will be light!

20

March 7

(. . .) Everything is going along fine here. Nothing new, as is usually the case in prison. Living with my fifty fellow inmates continues to be a rich and beneficial experience for me.[22] I am learning to belong more to others than to myself. Here no one claims priority or precedence. What belongs to one belongs to all. We have the whole day to listen to the radio, read, study, chat, and play bridge. But we must go to bed before one o'clock and get up before nine. I prefer to get to bed around eleven and to rise between 6:30 and 7:00, because I can organize my day better when I do. In time, you scarcely notice that you're in prison. It's as if we all had freely chosen this mode of life. The body adapts little by little, and we undergo surprising changes. After being in prison for awhile, there is nothing new to see or touch. But the sense of hearing gradually becomes more acute. We can recognize any outside noise, to the point of being able to tell the make of a car by its sound alone. We know instantly when the mess wagon has arrived and when the jailer is climbing the stairs to our cell. One sense quickens as another atrophies.

Sometimes I try to imagine what my life would be like under normal conditions. It would certainly be different now, after this experience in prison. For example, we've learned to eat everything with a spoon; we can handle it as if it were fork and knife too. Forks and knives aren't indispensable; they are a matter of habit. Nor do we need two dishes for a meal; the same plate serves for main course and dessert. We have learned to skin oranges with our hands as cleanly as if we had a knife. Till now I could never read lying down without soon getting sleepy and dropping the book. Now I can spend a whole day in bed reading without feeling the least bit sluggish. Our body adapts slowly but surely, without our noticing it. Our basic needs are reduced, and our physical resistance increases. Today I could live perfectly well with two pairs of pants and two shirts. Prison is a great education in this respect. It teaches one to live in community, to study in the midst of noise, to sleep with the light on (. . .).

21

To his brothers and sisters

March 7

(. . .) What a pleasant surprise Mom pulled on me last Wednesday! (. . .) I have already begun to celebrate Dad's birthday in my prayers. It seems to me that we have little to ask and much to be thankful for. What I love most in Dad is his youthful spirit. It is evident in his ability to grasp the new historical situation in which we are involved as agents. Having eight children requires him to have great understanding and inner serenity. He cannot permit himself a one-track mind, because each of his children has a different way of life. The important thing is that we all have the same vision of humanity and the world, a vision acquired from our upbringing. How we make that vision real, or how we struggle to make it real, depends on the opportunities that life affords each of us. When I was Leo's age,[23] I never expected to end up in prison. Today prison life is a reality of which I am proud.

(. . .) Today our case is supposed to have reached the Military Tribunal. I think we'll know something about how it's going before this month is over. There is continued support for us in Europe, as we learned from the Sunday edition of *O Estado de São Paulo*.[24] We also learned that Dad got the letter we sent him and was deeply moved.

Sunday we decided, among other things, to use up a little energy. We pushed all the beds to the back of the cell, used two beams to fashion a makeshift goal, rolled our socks into a goodsize ball, and played a game of soccer. But the ball was pretty small and the players numerous, so we had a kneeing free-for-all that left us all hobbling around for a day. I was the goalie on my team, which won despite the poor showing I made (. . .).

22

To his parents

March 8

(. . .) I simply can't understand why you haven't gotten the letter I wrote you. It must have gotten lost. I thank you for the Easter greetings and wish you the same. We are very close to each other, even though I cannot be with you in person to celebrate the feast.

(. . .) There is one less prisoner here in cell 7. Otavio Angelo (whom I lent my bed to when he arrived a month ago) is now in Mexico, freed in exchange for the Japanese consul.[25] He and Diogenes de Oliveira were in this prison.

If any of us gets around to writing his prison memoirs, the chapter on this particular stretch of confinement will be one of

29

the most interesting. We've lived through unforgettable experiences this week. Never has freedom seemed so easy or so alluring. But like in a game with many players and few winners, no one knew who would luck out.

We heard about the whole thing shortly after visiting hours on Wednesday, but we remained sceptical. The kidnappers had spirited away the consul without leaving any note in his car—as had been done, for example, in the kidnapping of the American ambassador. There was doubt and uncertainty surrounding the whole affair. Suspicion arose, voiced by the personnel of the Japanese consulate and propagated by the press, that the kidnapping might be the work of common criminals seeking a ransom. Our terrible tension, along with our hope, increased by the hour. If the kidnapping was a political protest, who would be selected for the exchange? From Wednesday to Sunday all the radios in our cell were left on, tuned to the various stations that were on the air. By Thursday the kidnappers' silence was getting on our nerves. People were chain-smoking, thinking and talking of nothing else. Finally we realized that there was nothing more for us to say, that we had exhausted every hypothesis, but we kept returning to the topic in the hope of uncovering some new angle. Thursday afternoon the radio reported that the kidnapping had been carried out to secure the release of a certain number of political prisoners in exchange for the consul. The kidnappers had surfaced.

Our cell teemed with hopeful expectation. Some of our fellow inmates, who would almost certainly be sentenced to more than twenty or thirty years in prison, were filled with a singular euphoria. They seemed transfigured as they thought of themselves free and safe outside the country. They literally quivered with the force of attraction that freedom exerts on all human beings. But we still had to find out which political organization had pulled off the kidnapping, how many names were on their list, and whose.

Many political prisoners are registered by the police as belonging to specific leftist organizations. Once the kidnappers declared who they were, we could at least begin to guess who

30

might be on their list for the exchange. But we still didn't know what criteria the kidnappers might use or whether they would demand the release of more prisoners than had the kidnappers of the American ambassador. That same afternoon our new sense of security was greatly diminished when we learned that the communiqué had been signed by Lucena of the VPR command and that he was only asking for the release of five political prisoners. Considering the critical legal situation of numerous prisoners, his demands seemed much too modest. From the fact that he had signed the communiqué, we deduced that his wife (who was later killed in a shootout with the police) would be one of the five prisoners in question and that at least three would be released from our prison. A number of VPR militants are imprisoned here. Otavio Angelo never expected to be included in the list because he is considered a member of the ALN.

The list of names was made public Friday afternoon. Otavio turned pale with emotion when he heard his name. He had only been in prison two months. The inclusion of Mother Maurina's name[26] was a big surprise. The first wave of emotion was followed by a general outburst of sheer joy. Otavio started packing his bag, expecting them to come for him at any moment. In the meantime we all joined in singing to celebrate his freedom. The prevailing joy was reminiscent of the evening before a general amnesty. Only the weariness caused by nervous tension allowed some of us to get to sleep that night. The radios were left on because the police could not find a prisoner whose code name was listed as Toledo. There was a fresh wave of hope and a new round of conjecture.

The next morning we learned that the kidnappers had proposed a new name in place of Toledo. It was Diogenes de Oliveira, a prisoner in cell 5 of our prison.

DOPS came around two in the afternoon to pick up the freed prisoners for their plane flight out of the country. We cheered them as they left, and they were deeply moved but tried to maintain an air of serenity and dignified pride.

A list of only five names had not left us too much scope for conjecture. Before it was released to the public, we had thought it might contain the names of those who had kidnapped the American ambassador and had subsequently been arrested. Two of them are here. Working on the same supposition, the mother of one of them had rushed here to say goodbye to her son. But we were conjecturing amid an unexpected and fast-moving turn of events.

This affair may have some impact on our trial. Contrary to our expectations the report of the investigation into our case has not yet been handed in to the Military Tribunal. I personally am in no hurry. In the letter Mom wrote me last week, I noted a certain concern over the adverse effect my arrest might have on our family. I would very much like you all to look at the whole matter from my point of view, from the point of view of faith, of surrender to God's will, of service to our people and to history (. . .).

23

To a community of nuns

March 10

Dear Friends, I am writing to thank you for the support you have given my family. I also want to thank you for your prayers and for the books you sent (. . .).

It is as if the whole situation confronting us today has been revealed to us, and we suddenly realize that this is the path Jesus has chosen for his church. *Lumen Gentium* leaves no room for doubt about that. Once we sat at table with the rich, frequented stately mansions, and shared the dais of the powerful. The time has come for us to turn to the poor and the persecuted, the fighters for justice, the prisons; for it is a time of oppression. We do not regret ending up behind bars if it is important for the sake of the gospel and the church.

Here among our cellmates—political prisoners and common prisoners—we have found the living image of Jesus Christ. For us prison is truly a *theological experience.* Only by actually living it can you get some idea of the richness it offers. You come to see why the Christian's way to glory leads through the cross. It is the logic of the Servant of Yahweh. Many prisoners have read the books you sent. The stories that impress them most are those of Moses, Jesus' trials, and Demetrius.[27] But they pose an interesting question: "Why is the church only now presenting things from this viewpoint?" Our answer is closely related to our explanation of the fact that Christians are only now ending up in prison.

Every day we read the book of Psalms. The military authorities have decided that we are no longer Christians, much less religious, so they don't let us celebrate Mass here, but they cannot stop us from praying. We recite the Psalms together daily. Some of our lay companions pray with us out of the same book. One, a native of India, reads the Psalms for half an hour every morning. It reminds me of Bonhoeffer, a member of the Underground and prisoner of the Nazis, who wrote that he had found the Psalms to be the best form of prayer. *Prison is a privileged place of "metanoia" and "koinonia."* There Saint Paul was tempered, there the apostles spent some time, the martyrs and mystics, like Saint John of the Cross, turned their cells into cages of divine love.

The reason is that, in prison, life is seen as if it were a photographic negative. A developed print, which takes full advantage of the play of light, can sometimes create a false picture of reality. We sometimes need raw reality to work out the full potentiality of what is real. *Daydreams and mere fancies gradually fall away when torture confronts us with the prospect of death.* When we discover the full depth and dimension of the inner person, the outer person diminishes. We realize that life comes down to a few basic needs and a few essential values. This reduction to our basic and primeval dimensions shows us that the one and only real vocation of human beings is to take part in the intimacy of God. The more we cling tooth and nail to suffering, the closer this intimacy becomes (because we cannot evade suffering, and the only way to overcome it is to confront it with as much courage as possible). Just as sickness helps us to realize the value of good health, so prison reveals the true worth of freedom.

There is a lot of useless freedom on the outside. We are free only when we commit ourselves to the risk of history, when we decide to intervene in reality in such a way that it will be transfigured by our actions. It may well be that right now our deeds constitute a mystery for some people. But don't the purest and most authentic realities spring from mystery? There is no other way. God could not remain metaphysically suspended over us. It was inevitable that he would immerse himself in history, that in revealing himself he would reveal us—and vice versa. Dialogue presupposes encounter. Christ is a part of history at the same time that he transcends it. Here the freedom of the Christian is completed and fulfilled. The Incarnation is followed by the Resurrection.

So we must tell our companions here that we will remain "subversives" as long as one human being remains oppressed. Our commitment is not to one specific form of government, to one ideology or labor organization. Our commitment is to man, whose dignity we recognize and proclaim as forcefully as it is denied. There's no doubt that purgatory must exist as the state of tension between love and indifference in which you have no possibility of choosing between them. God chooses for us. Sometimes he even chooses against our will, as he chose for the reluctant prophets and also, I am sure, for the seven Dominicans, two secular priests, and the Jesuit who are imprisoned here. The choice has been made for us. Turning back now would not be prudence; it would be treason. Our task and duty here behind bars is clear.

Pray that all this will turn out as God wills. Pray for those prisoners who have no one on their side and who can count only on the strength of their ideals. Explain our situation to the Christian community. From the "church in prison" we send you assurances of our confidence and friendship. Now is the Passion; the Resurrection will come after.

24

To a Brazilian nun

March 10

Dearest Sister Carmen, your biscuits made a great hit here. Thanks also for the letter, which shows that our sisters in the faith are truly in communion with us. We feel the effect of their prayers. How can we explain the joy we feel, the certainty that all this is part of God's plan of salvation.

The commemoration of the Passion draws near, and as I relive in my own body the experience of Jesus Christ, I ask myself why he has chosen prison as the way. Is it not the abode of criminals and alienated people?

God chose to identify himself with the poor and the oppressed, and the religious life arose out of a need to make this same identification. People must see in us an image of their Master, and therefore we should not be afraid to follow the way of the cross. Saint Paul is a magnificent example: His apostolic journeys took him from one prison to another. Thus we learn to suffer joyfully and to die believing in life.

I believe, Sister, that we have acted according to the Spirit. I can say that without being presumptuous. We do not fear the justice of human beings because it cannot deprive us of anything, least of all the inner freedom that the Lord is now giving us.

A big hug to you and your community. Pray for us and our fellow prisoners.

Yours in expectation of the Resurrection.

25

To his parents

March 23

(. . .) Your courage in facing up to reality and your confidence in the future gives me much courage. At times, to tell you the truth, I become annoyed with myself for causing you so much anxiety. Then I realize that something else is involved here, that it has to do with the natural desire we all have to regain our freedom. But what is freedom? It is a question I frequently ask myself. There is the freedom that is based on money and the labor of others, and then there is the freedom of the human being who finds himself by giving himself, by service to others. Were the great men of history, such as Julius Caesar and Napoleon Bonaparte, free only because they did not owe obedience to anyone? Jesus Christ and Francis of Assisi chose the path of self-sacrifice, of service to others, of absolute obedience. Were they free?

In a study of freedom in the present-day world, Marcuse states that one can hardly find a free person in the United States. Yet that country is regarded as the model of freedom in the Western world. There is a high degree of social organization, resulting from the breakneck speed of a technological advance in which people are conditioned by the machine. Because of this the industrial and governmental systems strictly control the individual. The choices available to average Americans are extremely limited. They can pick a make of a car, a particular plane flight, a brand of film, or a six-pack of beer. But they have little chance to choose some alternative to the "American way of life." And despite deep-rooted religious sentiments and patterns of conduct, Americans lack spiritual depth and philosophical objectivity. They do not question or ponder their existence, much less consider changing the status quo; quite the contrary, they seek to propagate it. The results of American freedom are plainly to be seen in the newspapers: a persistent and spreading plague in Southeast Asia and the Middle East, the world's record consumption of toxic drugs, unbridled eroticism, artistic productions devoid of any constructive content (like the Hollywood productions that teach you nothing but to drink Coca-Cola), racial segregation, and so on. Such technological freedom was well analyzed and criticized by Aldous Huxley in *Brave New World*.

Even less can you talk about freedom under regimes ruled by the likes of Hitler and Stalin, where all power comes from the state and is exercised exclusively in its name, where the people are all but excluded from the political process and dissidents are imprisoned, outlawed, or killed.

The fundamental point of these examples is the fact that the state can restrict or take away freedom but can never confer it. *For freedom is something that must be won.* People must continually fight for it, even at the cost of their lives.

I believe that freedom, as a societal achievement, has not yet come into existence. So far there have been occasional moments of freedom, areas of freedom, free individuals. But freedom as a condition of life has not yet come into being. Slavery as a legal status was abolished only a century ago. But people go on creating new myths to compensate for their frustrations—new forms of subjugation, like colonialism and imperialism. The very social structure in which we live is fundamentally coercive. From the moment we come into the world we are taught what we "must not" do, we are subjected to repressive laws, and we can see a policeman on every corner. The existing social structure so exacerbates this condition that many human beings do not know what to make of freedom even when they have a chance to be free.

A century ago humankind began to discover itself through psychology, sociology, and biology. But we are still too much "outside" ourselves. We have made little use of the psychic and spiritual riches within us. I believe we will attain true freedom only when we arrive at the stage of evolution that Teilhard de Chardin calls the "noosphere," the realm of the spirit. Surely the spirit will be the last great discovery of humankind. Then we will be free because freedom will exist, first and foremost, within us.

The witness of free human beings helps us to believe in freedom and desire it. Real freedom develops inside us and radiates outward. No prison can destroy it. I have received this kind of witness from my cellmates, from children, from poets and saints, and from the poor. They are people who cannot be imprisoned by bars. They speak with their eyes, with their silences, and with their serenity. They are prophets of the spirit, who know how to lay hold of the reins of history. It is they who are really dangerous, who should be feared above all others by those who don't wish to hear the word "freedom" or admit its existence.

It's to be expected that since I'm a prisoner, I should speak of freedom. I do so because every day I discover it within myself and my cellmates and realize its value and its price (. . .).

37

26

Holy Thursday

(. . .) As we see it, the causes and consequences of our imprisonment can only be analyzed in the light of God's word. By it we can see their fullest and truest significance. In the light of God's word we can grasp the prophetic dimension of our "affair"[29] as it relates to the church in Latin America. This is especially true if we consider it in dialectical terms. Indeed I think this is the standpoint from which we should interpret the message of creation and promise, of fall and pardon, of historicity and salvation, of incarnation and resurrection, that make up the main strands of the Bible. It seems to me that the fundamentalist and historicist interpretations that have prevailed so far are not valid. Biblical exegetes have never managed to dissociate themselves from a priori principles regarding the biblical test. They look to the Bible for a confirmation of *their own* truth, not for the truths contained in revelation itself. Or else they start from etiological and infrastructural descriptions—the more recent approach—but even this method is not free from substantive defects. For if excessive value is placed on just one element of the infrastructure, this can invalidate the overall interpretation.

I readily admit my ignorance in the field of exegesis. This is no false modesty, just an easily verifiable fact. But I'm much inclined to take the risk of making a mistake, that is, of being overly subjective, because I feel sure that I will know how to correct such a mistake if necessary. Prison places us Christians in a situation of continuing dialogue with other people of very different tendencies from ours. A cell like this one, where fifty people are gathered together, imposes on us a community life quite different from the one we are used to in our religious houses. Here there are no basic assumptions by which to define positions or delineate the boundaries between different faiths; and here there is no room for fear of one another. It's confrontation and debate at every moment, and the only valid response is our life itself. But our cellmates do have great curiosity about Christianity, and it becomes obvious that our language is inadequate to express clearly who and what we are—in contrast to their language, by the way. It is also clear that in a deeper way than us they are living certain values that we had thought were the exclusive possession of Christians raised in the theological virtues. Their appeal is strong, our response limited. For example, we are lost in astonished admiration at the witness of a young atheist here who is willing to accept martyrdom in the name of a hope rather than in the name of a faith.

That's why we feel the need to go back to the Bible, to discard present theology, and to figure out the changes that are urgently needed in our Christian language. How are we to interpret God's plan in the Bible and in history? How are we to bear witness to the unity of so divided a church? What do we have to offer to people whose courageous witness is a silent challenge to us? When have our theological reflections dealt with crucial problems of the present day? What do we have to say before events run their own course? I would like some bishops and theologians to spend at least a month in prison. There they might discover a reality that few of us experience and none of us discuss: *that grace is not the exclusive property of Christians but God's gift to any human being whatsoever.*

To get back to my initial subject, it's becoming evident to me that our Christian interpretations of the Bible and of history are not particularly true to the facts or to contemporary language. For example, the true story of Francis of Assisi has not yet been written. What we have so far is hagiography dripping with illuminism or plaintive piety or outright folklore. There is precious little truth in it. Francis of Assisi is turned into a medieval case history, and so he loses all his relevance and value for us, precisely because we cannot relate his life and deeds to the historical and structural conditions in which we are living today.

Clear proof of all this can be found in the unsuccessful attempt of Vatican II to express itself in an idiom intelligible to modern people. I reread the conciliar documents while I was preparing my court defense. It struck me that they sound fine to people who are used to scholastic terminology but have little to say to secularized non-Christians. Just try to explain them to a Marxist! They were supposed to have been incisive and crystal-clear, like a manifesto. Instead we end up with a conglomeration of paragraphs in which every statement is preceded by a repetition of the relevant articles of faith—as if they were afraid that something might be read or interpreted out of context. *Gaudium et Spes,* for example, which starts from an anthropological perspective, quickly gets lost in the repetition of dogmatic truths. It sticks to defining principles and never gets to practical guidelines. When will we find something to say about real life that will be more than the usual mumbo jumbo?

We must scrape the rust off theology, which has been dominated by stagnation since the Middle Ages. For three or four centuries we have been absorbing the thought of Thomas Aquinas without ever seeing what it signified for theological reflection in its own day. Confronted with the Renaissance and its innovative currents, we retreated—except for Luther, who had the courage to move forward. Confronted with the industrial revolution, we hurled anathemas. And in the face of scientific progress, we simply voice suspicion.

We haven't shown the daring of the church Fathers, of men like Augustine and Thomas Aquinas, who thought in theological terms about their own times. Only now are we beginning to wake up, very slowly, from a long dogmatic slumber. With Karl Rahner and moral theology, we may now have caught up with Kant. We still have to get past Hegel and when we do there will be many surprises. Now is the time for us to do what Thomas Aquinas did. He had the courage to take his lead from the philosophy of Aristotle. We must have the courage to give serious attention to the questions and contributions that Marxism has to offer to theology. We must try to harmonize the intellectual currents of our day just as Clement of Rome and Justin Martyr did in their day.

Well, Pedro, these are the ramblings of a prisoner who doesn't have many books around for backup support. We have just a few here. They bring us books from the monastery, but the censor often prohibits certain volumes. For example, we can't have books by Bultmann, Cullmann, or Cox. Perhaps it's precisely this lack of books, along with the many hours we have free for brain work, that leads us to reconsider the Christian life. I recall Bonhoeffer's experience and, on another level, Dostoyevsky's. Both spent time behind bars. Perhaps the interest of European Christians in Marxism grew out of the time they shared in the Resistance movement and in concentration camps.

When you have time, I would like you to write me something about the book of Job. Ernst Bloch wrote something about it, I think, when discussing atheism in the Bible. I'd be very curious to read that book, but I don't know if it's been translated into French. And Bonhoeffer mentions his love for the Psalms, particularly Psalms 3, 37, and 70, in *Letters and Papers from Prison*. If you can find the translations, please send them to me.

I wish you an Easter full of liberation. Never have I lived it so intensely, because this year I am living through the passion in my own flesh. Unfortunately, the military authorities won't let us experience it liturgically. We remain united with you and your community in this vigil of freedom, and I embrace you in hope and friendship.

27

To his brother Tony[30]

March 28

Dear Tony, your letter made me very happy. I particularly liked your drawing of the comet and the Easter egg. It's obvious that you are coming along in your studies.

I didn't have a chance to see the comet. That morning I got up at 5:00 A.M. to see it, but the sky was covered with clouds and I couldn't see any stars. Someday the comet will return, and we'll see it together. This time it passed by quickly because

God sent it to take a quick look at the world and see how we human beings are doing. It came early, while people were still sleeping, to make a quick inspection of the earth. But it didn't see any of the wars or starvation or fights—none of the bad things—because people were sleeping peacefully in their beds. It only saw the eyes of children who had stayed awake all night to see it. And the children's eyes were full of light and joy. So the comet toured the world, looking at children's eyes all over the world. It probably saw the almond eyes of little Japanese children too. Then it returned to God. But it didn't find God in heaven. It knew that God had come down to live in the hearts of children and poor people. So it sent news to God that everything was going fine on earth, that people were super, and that they weren't doing anything wrong. God was satisfied and told the comet that it could have a year's vacation before returning to earth. So the comet decided to take a vacation around Mars.

Happy Easter! The child Jesus lives in your heart. A big bear hug and a kiss to you from your brother.

28

To Pedro

March 28

Dear Friend, your letter was a great joy to all of us. It made us feel that we're not alone in this adventure and that our experience does have some positive value for the gospel.

That is enough to justify our imprisonment here. It's not important to know how long we're going to be here. The important thing is what will come of this seed sown in prison. Perhaps our real charism is to offer Christian witness behind bars, following in the footsteps of Saint Paul, who went from one prison to another. But only God knows that for sure. We are at peace because we know that we're following the path Jesus Christ marked out for his church. All the apostles experienced martyrdom. The primitive church wrote its history in prisons, with the blood that had been spilled in torture. Today we're offering a witness of hope, as well as faith, in the sense of being present to events in the world. From the moment that we discovered the eschatological dimension of revelation and theology, the historical perspective of our hope has been leading us here to prison.

When I first got to prison and was put in solitary confinement, I thought for a whole month that I would never get out alive. But I felt real joy at the thought that I was sacrificing myself for a hope. In other words I came to realize that the promise made to us in Abraham and Jesus is ineluctable. That promise is what gives our struggle its guarantee. I know that it isn't easy for the Christian community to accept what is happening now as the *normal thing*—without self-pity or perplexity, but rather with joy. But we only have to remember that in an earlier time Christians were called "atheists" and "disturbers of the peace." They were accused of idolatry, of holding orgies and sacrificing human flesh at their eucharistic gatherings. Today, unfortunately, many Christians think that Christianity is a "social order," rather than an attitude of questioning and protest within history. They tend to forget that Christians aren't obligated to particular ideologies, political parties, or historical projects, but rather to the task of fashioning the future where the kingdom lies. To this end, Christians can adopt particular convictions, but they must always be provisional and questioning, in this sense: that so long as there is one oppressed human being in the world, the Christian will confront, question, and combat this oppression.

At times this Christian attitude may coincide with a particular political conviction. That's to be expected as long as we live on earth and amid the events of history. You can't put your hand in water without getting it wet. There is no redemption without risk. For other Christians, though, faith is nothing but a code of middle-class morality that requires marital fidelity, going to Mass on Sunday, and praying to God when you're in trouble. These people believe in a God "above" and don't realize that God can be truly known only in Jesus Christ. Jesus Christ is the presence of God in history. This man had the

43

courage to break with the morality of the Pharisees in his preaching and his way of life. He challenged the established order and was condemned to death as an "agitator."

I met you last year in June at São Leopoldo, when you were teaching at Christus Sacerdos.[31] I was your student for a few hours when you gave that conference on contemporary religious life at the request of Father Mueller (a man transfigured by grace). I read your notes on the changes that took place in the transition from a cosmocentric religious mentality to a secularized anthropocentric mentality. Let's talk a little about this.

It's true that the phenomenon of secularization is evident on a worldwide scale. It's the product of the industrial revolution, which caused a cultural revolution. But I am also convinced that secularization, interpreted in these terms, applies only to a highly developed technological society, like Europe or North America. It is undeniable that people today no longer view the world in religious terms and that their thrust toward autonomy becomes more and more evident. But I am afraid that certain authors want to *transform Christianity into a product that will sell well.* There is no doubt that talking on the telephone and driving an automobile and shopping at the supermarket and playing bridge on Saturday night have something to do with faith in God—that in these acts we either draw closer to God or move further away from him. It is also true that being close to God does not require acts of heroism, prolonged fasting, all-night vigils, or imprisonment. We must certainly rid ourselves of the notion that holiness is something exceptional, something fashioned out of extraordinary deeds and moments. But we cannot forget that Christianity is the awareness of a promise and that this awareness presupposes certain basic attitudes toward history. So what is involved, it seems to me, is not just a new secularized mentality and a new language to deal with the problem of God. Also involved is the existentially eschatological meaning of Christianity.

What does Jesus mean when he says that we are not of the world? Or Paul, when he says we must not conform to the world? To me they are saying that Christianity means nonconformity with the *saeculum*, with the here and now of history. They aren't referring to the planet earth as such. So we are not a secularized presence in history; rather, we are the irruption of the divine into secular society. I prefer to speak of the secularization of Christians, not the secularization of the world, insofar as Christians proclaim and bear witness to the eschatological promise. For only we, thanks to divine revelation, have any certainty about what does not yet exist, about the presence of God who has broken into human history.

So it makes sense to talk about secularization in a church that had shut itself up in the sacred. But I'm afraid that secularization will become only a problem of language, of mentality and habits, with a view to adapting to the *saeculum*. The *saeculum* aspires to the sacred, and our presence in it signifies challenge and protest and questioning—never conformity. That is why Christianity is the religion of the poor, of the proletariat, of the exploited class that is always the negation of the established order. The middle class can see Christianity only as an individualistic morality, because their concern is to maintain the status quo, which they call "Christian," as if Christianity were a force for resisting the dynamism of history. By the very nature and structure of their outlook, on the other hand, the poor are better able to receive and live the gospel, because nothing ties them to the here and now. Precisely because of their inner freedom, the poor are filled with hope and expectation, with a will to change and an incomparable capacity for sacrifice, service, and love. But we must present them with a Christianity that is praxis and not just a body of doctrines and liturgical gestures. The person who undergoes conversion cannot continue to live as before.

I hope to talk more about this praxis in my next letter to you. Please take what I've said as opinion, not as certainty. The only certainty is the uncertainty of our questioning. Regards to your community. Pray for our companions here in prison, anonymous martyrs of hope. Celebrate Mass for us, since the military authorities will not let us. In joy.

29

March 29

My Dear Friends, I wish you all the happiness I feel on this day of the Resurrection. The season is sharing my joy because the day has been bright, blue, and full of life. At dawn we sang and prayed for everything in us and around us that is making the passover from sorrow to joy, from prison to freedom, from uninvolvement to struggle, from death to life. Together we read several passages of the New Testament, particularly the letters St. Paul wrote from prison. Then we divided a huge Easter egg among us. It was as big as a football and filled with chocolates. Coqueiro strummed the guitar, while the members of our makeshift choir sang and the rest kept time with spoons, pots, and pans. The only sadness was the absence of Giorgio,[32] who is probably living the Passion in his own body at DOPS.

I'm sure that this is the Holy Week I have lived most intensely. Placed in a situation similar to Christ's, we participate more vividly and truly in his sufferings. They are prolonged in us: "Hard-pressed on every side, we are never hemmed in; bewildered, we are never at our wits' end; hunted, we are never abandoned to our fate; struck down, we are not left to die. Wherever we go we carry death with us in our body, the death that Jesus died, that in this body also life may reveal itself, the life that Jesus lives" (2 Cor 4:8–10).

Easter, which is liberation, has not yet arrived for us, who are prisoners in Christ. It is important that it arrive first for the church, that our imprisonment help to liberate God's word from every kind of subjugation and compromise. That is our mission, and we shouldn't grieve over it. It must be carried out to the end.

But all this is also an occasion of joy for us. We rejoice that we are able to suffer for Christ, that we can trust in him who has promised us victory. His resurrection bears witness to that victory. What good would our faith be if Christ had not been

46

raised from the dead? Today I see my life as something very small in space and time. It acquires significance solely in the context of death and resurrection (. . .).

30

To Pedro

March 29

Dear Pedro, a happy Easter to you and your community. May it truly be a passover toward freedom on the long road before us.

It's not a matter of winning, but simply of regaining the ground lost by a church tied into money, prestige, and power. Because of this alliance the church didn't have to work for a living and resided in palatial mansions. Now the church is turning toward the poor, toward their yearnings and their struggles. Now it is working for a living, and so it is calumniated, maltreated, and put into prison. That's the way it has always been in history, and that's how it will always be. We are a part of the church living in prison. We don't give in to discouragement or surrender. We're grateful and happy to be here in this situation. We face insecurity, calumny, and torture; but we also experience unity, solidarity, constant prayer, and deepening charity. Our life depends solely on hope and on the complete support of our families and the most aware members of the church. All this is precious, and we keep going back to reflect on its essential elements. We ponder the reality of life, eternal life, and of death, which is the precondition for life. It is the mystery of Christ's death and resurrection: What matters is life, but death is the pathway to it. Once again we're in the novitiate, to begin anew. Never have I felt more like a priest offering sacrifice or like a religious offering witness. I can only convey a hint of our hope. It's impossible to say it all. A big hug to you and the others.

47

31

Dear Pedro, we got the notes you sent us. They'll be a big help to us, and we'll use them as a foundation for our own thinking. We have the facts, or rather, we are the facts, and your notes will help us understand them in the light of faith. Our prison experience is too important to be restricted to a few people in a short time. It will take much sorrow and sacrifice before the church as a whole manages to purify itself sufficiently to assimilate this experience, which belongs not only to us who are physically imprisoned here, but really to the whole church. Right now the church is dumbfounded, but in time it will understand and respond to the sacrifice of Christ.

We have been happy here, as if in a new and unexpected novitiate. There are fifty of us in a cell hardly big enough for twenty. We have only one shower. The atrocious condition of this prison has been reported to the judge of the Civil Court. We have tried to improve things: We do our own cooking; we try to keep the cell sanitary; our families bring us food; we make up pastimes; we "improve our minds"; we pray and study theology. We don't let ourselves give in to desperation, and we find ourselves being restored continually (. . .).

32

To his parents

March 31

Dearest Mom and Dad, I would be very happy if you could look at everything that is happening to me from my own point of view, which is the point of view of faith, of abandonment to God's plans, of service to our people, to history. We were born and raised in a middle-class environment, where you always have to preserve appearances. By now I could have had my B.A. and been earning a good salary on some newspaper, secure in the esteem and admiration that certain people had for me before they learned what choices I've made. But none of that has anything to do with my vocation as a Christian. History is not built on appearances but on choices. You have to choose, and you can't please two opposing sides. Either you align yourself with the poor and the oppressed, or you acquire the badge of the oppressor. You have to live either by human logic and common sense or by the impulses of the Spirit.

I know how hard it is to live for the future. Those who live in the past and wish at all cost to preserve the present (as if they could) do all they can to destroy us. They heap lies, abuse, and threats on us, and they take away our freedom. But they can't make us stumble into contradictions. We must be courageous and consistent. We must commit ourselves to the future because God's promises are there. The book of Genesis tells us that Abraham, out of faith in God's promise, forsook his native land and his wealth to journey to the promised land, a land flowing with milk and honey. That journey symbolizes the attitude of the Christian. Jesus came to proclaim the kingdom of justice and peace to us. Each of us in our own way, according to the abilities we have been given, contributes to the making of this kingdom and the quest for it. The kingdom can not be established outside history, so our journey toward it must take place within history (. . .).

33

To Marco, a student friend

April 7

Dear Marco, those who know that they have to stay here a long time are more relaxed. They follow a schedule, a program of study, and so they continue to live their lives. They don't waste time recalling the past or dreaming of some imminent, utopian future. They integrate their activities into the rhythm of life that you can establish in prison. As far as our personal life is concerned, the rhythm of prison life can be as intense

49

and productive as our pattern of living outside. Idleness is the most dangerous temptation facing a prisoner. It is what turns prison into a school for crime for ordinary prisoners. Lacking any formal education and unable to devote himself to reading, the average inmate spends the whole day sleeping, rehashing the past, and talking nonsense. Abandoned to his own uselessness, he wears himself out day by day. (There is no chance for rehabilitation because our prison system is punitive rather than corrective.) His only prospect is to learn new techniques of theft and crime from his cellmates.

We can hear the conversations in the other cell block. They shout to each other from cell to cell, always in underworld slang and never using their real names. They use nicknames so that there is no danger of being informed on. (. . .) If one of them doesn't have a nickname, he is labelled by the place he comes from. They usually sleep all day and sing all evening, banging out the rhythm of their songs. (. . .) The most curious thing of theirs is the *teresa*. It's a looped string that they use to pass objects from one cell to another. If a person can handle the *teresa* well, he can do wondrous feats. For example, a prisoner may throw a cigarette down the corridor, so that it stops right in front of the intended recipient. But then a prisoner in another cell shoots out his *teresa* and lassoes it for himself. Another easily learned technique is sign language. If you want to talk to someone at night, you use sign language so you don't wake up other prisoners (. . .).

34

To a community of nuns

April 7

(. . .) Our lawyer came to see us. He had no news about our trial. He told us that the public prosecutor, Durval Airton de Moura, was studying it "attentively and sympathetically." In general, the handling of cases in the Second Tribunal is a slow process. There are people arrested a year ago who are only now being interrogated. If our cases are heard in the order in which we were arrested we will not come to trial before next year.

It's a curious thing that after you have spent a certain amount of time in prison, your lawyer has nothing new to say when he comes. He functions much like a doctor at the bedside of a chronically ill patient. All he can offer is consolation. He has no remedies to offer. He can try to give some idea of the complicated juridical and penal mechanisms and how they work, and he can try to lighten our pessimism a bit. Many people look for a confessor, not to be pardoned but to unburden themselves. Even though our lawyer can't function directly in the trial process, the very fact that we know he exists and that he comes here is a source of great comfort.

The other day I was talking to the mother of M.C., my companion in prison who is presently on trial in Rio, charged with participating in the kidnapping of the U.S. ambassador. (There, it seems, he confessed that he was the one who struck the ambassador on the head with a gun butt. He never told us that.) I have always been greatly impressed by this woman's composure in the face of her son's imprisonment. In Rio some officials tried to shake her by saying that M. would be sentenced to death or life imprisonment. She answered very calmly: "That does not bother me. It is as if my son had cancer. However much people try, they cannot find a cure today. But perhaps we will discover one very soon. In any case being in prison is better than having cancer."

To change the subject, we have sent the TV back. I'm glad because now we have at least a little quiet in the cell after supper (. . .).

All of us here thank you for the Easter greetings. You are always in our prayers. Pray for all prisoners, especially for those who are living the Passion of Jesus Christ in their own flesh. A big hug to you all.

51

35

April 7

(. . .) It's gotten cold, and now it's hard to get out of bed in the morning. I get up around 6:30 A.M. and devote an hour to yoga. It's the best thing I've discovered here in prison. N., who is a yoga teacher, is a fellow prisoner in our cell. Every day he directs my exercises. We're divided into two groups, one exercising at nine, the other at ten. I prefer to get up early and do the exercises by myself, because I have more time available to me then. Yoga movements are supposed to be very slow, and it's all based on breathing. Traditional gymnastics help build up the muscles, but yoga helps develop endurance, makes the body supple, increases our control over our bodies, and develops concentration, emotional balance, and sound health. Another advantage is that it isn't tiring, because all the movements are slow and follow the rhythm of normal breathing. Little by little I'm learning to correct a whole series of mistakes that we inflict on our bodies. You should never breathe with your mouth and lungs; you should breathe with your nose and diaphragm. I've stopped using a pillow, and I'm learning to rest for a few minutes with my head down because it's a mistake not to let blood flow to the brain. Over time these mistakes may help to cause arteriosclerosis. My nervous tension disappears if I manage to concentrate for a few minutes, interrupting my breathing and then resuming its normal rhythm. In this way I correct the cardiac alterations provoked by emotion or fear and completely regain a sense of tranquility. In short I'm finding yoga to be a wonderful source of all kinds of miracles. I need only mention that it allows its practitioners in the Himalayas to walk around naked in the snow and control their body temperature by their breathing (. . .).

Once again we hear that we'll be transferred to Taubate next month. Nothing is certain right now, but it could happen. That would be the fourth prison I would get to know (. . .).